At last – a collection of totally sensible jokes!

Includes 'Household Tips', Old Proverbs, Restaurant Guide, Sensible Things to Say, Serious Film Quiz, A Special Section on Frogs, Serious News Items, 'Cookery Corner' – and MUCH, MUCH MORE!

Guaranteed free of Knock Knock jokes! (Almost . . .)

DR. DRIVEL'S SERIOUS ⋆ Joke Book ⋆

Brough Girling

Illustrated by Jonathan Allen

RED FOX

A Red Fox Book

Published by Random Century Children's Books
20 Vauxhall Bridge Road, London SW1V 2SA

A division of the Random Century Group

London Melbourne Sydney Auckland
Johannesburg and agencies throughout the world

First published 1991

Text © Brough Girling 1991
Illustrations © Jonathan Allen 1991

The right of Brough Girling and Jonathan Allen to be identified as the author and illustrator of this work respectively has been asserted by them in accordance with the Copyright, Designs and Patents Act, 1988.

This book is sold subject to the condition that it shall not, by way of trade or otherwise, be lent, resold, hired out, or otherwise circulated without the publisher's prior consent in any form of binding or cover other than that in which it is published and without a similar condition including this condition being imposed on the subsequent purchaser.

Set in Century Schoolbook
Typeset by JH Graphics Ltd, Reading

Printed and bound in Great Britain by
Cox & Wyman Ltd, Reading

ISBN 0 09 979190 0

Contents

Introduction	7
Doctor Drivel's Really *Serious* Guide to Sensible things to Say	9
Doctor Drivel's Hand-picked Selection of *Serious* Riddles	12
Doctor Drivel's *Serious* List of Favourite Things	16
Sensible Heroes and Heroines	20
Doctor Drivel's Very Special, *Serious* Film Quiz	23
Doctor Drivel's Miscellany of *Serious* Jokes	24
Doctor Drivel's Old Proverbs	27
Doctor Drivel's Sensible Household Tips	29
Seriously Puzzling Thoughts	33
Doctor Drivel's *Serious* Sports Special	36
Now For Something Really *Serious*	39
Doctor Drivel at the Art Gallery	42
A Further Collection of Even More *Serious* Jokes	44
Doctor Drivel's Doggorn Sensible Jokes	47
Yet More *Serious* Jokes	50
Doctor Drivel's don't Get Cross Selection	53

Serious Animal Corner	57
Doctor Drivel's Guide to *Serious* Tourists	59
Doctor Drivel's Guide to Frogs	61
The Writing's not on the Wall	63
Doctor Drivel's Sensible Children's Corner	65
Mummy, Mummy, There's Something *Seriously* Wrong	67
Doctor Drivel's Very Own Sensible Knock Knock Jokes	69
Here is the News	70
Doctor Drivel's Own List of *Seriously* Sensible Things to do	73
One of the Most *Serious* Topics in the World – Teachers	75
Doctors! – Oh No, How Serious	77
Doctor Drivel Asks a Very Sensible Question: What Do You Call . . . ?	82
Doctor Drivel's Christmas Crackers	87
Doctor Drivel's *Serious* Restaurant Guide	89
Serious Book Titles	91
Doctor Drivel's *Serious* Cookery Corner	92

Introduction

Doctor Drivel is Professor of Serious Jokes at the Humour Department of Limerick University.

He has made a life long study of what you get when you cross certain things, why other things cross the road, and what you call certain people.

This book contains all the sensible things he knows. He hopes you will seriously enjoy it.

Doctor Drivel's Really *Serious* Guide to Sensible Things to Say

A car driven by a learner driver drove off the road and straight into a lake.

'What did you do that for?' asked the instructor firmly, stepping out into the water.

'You told me to dip my lights,' replied the learner, sensibly.

If you ever go to a ballet, it's really sensible to stand up half way through the first half and shout, 'Could you speak up, please? We can't hear you at the back!'

What does your father do?
Sensible answer: *Well, he used to own a paper shop, but it blew away.*

Sensible Indian Smoke Signal:

This means: *Help, my blanket is on fire!*

If a policeman arrests you and says 'I must warn you that anything you say may be taken down . . .', it's fairly sensible to say, 'Your trousers.'

If another policeman stops your car and says, 'Excuse me, Sir, are you aware that this is a one way street?', the sensible answer is 'But, Officer, I was only going one way!'

If you are ever taken to court and have to take the oath, when the Usher says 'say after me . . .', it's essential to immediately reply 'After me!'.

Doctor Drivel's Hand-picked Selection of *Serious* Riddles

What's black and white and eats like a horse?
A zebra, stupid.

What do American Indians put under their arms?
Scalpum powder.

What's stupid and flies to the moon?
A loony module.

What did the policeman say to his belly button?
You're under a vest.

How does an eskimo keep the roof on his house?
'e glues it.
[**Please note:** An eskimo's house with no toilet is an ig.]

What's yellow and white and travels at a hundred miles an hour?
A train driver's egg sandwich.

Where do pigs live in New York?
Sty-scrapers.

What do you get if you cross an elephant with a box of laxative pills?
Out of the way.

What's yellow and flickers?
A banana with a loose connection.

Who invented the first aeroplane that didn't work?
The Wrong Brothers.

What do you call two robbers?
A pair of knickers.

I suppose they get intruder window . . .

Why do cows lie down when it rains?
To keep each udder dry.

What do you get if you put a blow lamp down a rabbit hole?
Hot cross bunnies.

Why is an owl cleverer than a chicken?
Have you ever heard of Kentucky fried owl?

Can you jump higher than the Eiffel Tower?
Sure, the Eiffel Tower can't jump.

How do you make a Maltese cross?
Stamp on his foot.

What kind of umbrella does Kylie Mynogue use when it rains?
A wet one.

What did Humpty do with his hat?
Humpty dumped his hat on a wall.
[**Please note:** This joke is more serious when sung.]

What's green and brown and would kill you if it jumped out of a tree on to you?
A snooker table.

Doctor Drivel's *Serious* List of Favourite Things

What's a cat's favourite breakfast cereal?
Mice Crispies.
[**Please note:** Witches like snap cackle and pop.]

> Actually my favourite food is soup in a basket.

What's a bat's favourite song?
Rain drops keep falling on my feet.

What's a ghost's favourite airline?
British Scareways, they really like the Air Ghostesses – and particularly enjoying flying to the Isle of Fright.
[**Please note:** the in-flight meal should be scream of mushroom soup.]

A parrot's favourite food is Polly-filla.

Ghosts like ghoulash.

Dracula likes nectarines.

A frog's favourite drink is Croaka Cola.

Dr Jekyll's favourite game was Hyde and seek.

A crocodile likes playing Snap.

A cat's favourite TV programme is Miami Mice.

Ducks' TV favourites include duckumentaries, or the feather forecast.

A horse's favourite TV programme is *Neigh*bours.

Their favourite sport is stable tennis.

Sensible Heroes and Heroines

Davy Crockett was a sensible hero because he had three ears.
Three ears?
Yes, a left ear, a right ear, and a wild front ear.

Batman must be really sensible – he wears his underpants on top of his trousers!

Serious question: Were the Invisible Man's mum and dad his transparents?

What is big and hairy and flies to America?
King Kongcorde.

> I go to the bank to see the Loan Arranger.

The Lone Ranger came over a hill and saw Tonto lying near a cactus bush with his ear to the ground.

'Keemo Sabi,' said the masked stranger's friend, 'a stage coach has just passed this way, pursued by Indians, it had four horses, the front one was white and the one at the back on the left was slightly lame.'

'That's amazing Tonto!' said the Lone Ranger, 'How can you tell all that?'

'They just ran over me,' replied his friend.
[**Please note:** These days Lone Ranger drives a Lone Range Rover.]

What goat is a hero of the wild west?
Billy the Kid.

What gum does J.R. use?
Ewing gum.

Doctor Drivel's Very Special, *Serious* Film Quiz

1. How do we know that the girl in Jaws had dandruff?
2. What film title was inspired by a tin of baked beans?
3. What film is about people who steal watch dogs?
4. What bald actor played 007?
5. In the film Snow White, which song is about getting holiday snaps back from the chemist?

Answers

1. She left her head and shoulders on the beach
2. Gone With the Wind
3. Raiders of the Lost Bark
4. Shorn Connery
5. 'Some day my prints will come'

Doctor Drivel's Miscellany of *Serious* Jokes

MAN: 'My girlfriend is one of twins.'
HIS FRIEND: *'Can you tell them apart?'*
MAN: 'Yes, her brother's got a beard.'

I met my girlfriend in a revolving door — we've been going around together ever since.

A man went into a butcher's shop and asked the butcher, 'Have you got any mince?'
The butcher gave him a Polo.

Another man went into a butcher's shop and said, 'Can I have some pieces for my dog?'
'Sure,' said the butcher, 'Which bits is he missing?'

A man was trying to cross a very busy main road. 'There's a zebra crossing just round this corner,' a kind policeman remarked to him.
'Is there!' said the man grumpily, 'I hope he's having more luck than I am.'

A tramp came up to a rich-looking woman. 'Spare me a few quid, Madam,' he said. 'I haven't had a bite all day.'

'Oh dear,' said the lady. Then she bit him.

A man knocked on a lady's door. 'Excuse me, Madam, I've come to mend your door bell.'

'But you should have been here last week!'

'Oh, I came: I kept ringing the bell but no one answered!'

LADY: I'd like a bar of soap please.
SHOP ASSISTANT: *Certainly, Madam, would you like it scented?*
LADY: No, I'll take it with me.

A man went into a pet shop. 'I'd like some bird seed, please.'

'Certainly, Sir,' said the man behind the counter, 'What birds do you have?'

'Well, none – I haven't planted the seeds yet!'

GIRL: 'My dad is very stingy. Last Christmas he gave my mum some flowers?'
FRIEND: *'That's not stingy; what sort of flowers?'*
GIRL: 'We don't know, they haven't come up yet!'

A man knocked on a farmer's door. 'I'm very sorry,' he said to the farmer's wife, 'But I've just run over one of your chickens. Could I replace it?'

'Certainly,' said the farmer's wife, 'How many eggs do you lay a week?'

Doctor Drivel's Old Proverbs

Old fishermen never die, they just smell that way.

Never try to hang a man with a wooden leg — you can't tie a knot in it.

He who crosses an elephant with a hearth rug, gets a very big pile on his carpet.

Someone who can't tell chalk from cheese seldom gets his sandwiches nicked.

People who live in glass houses shouldn't take their clothes off before it gets dark.

Don't cross your chickens before they're burnt.

Don't waste wood – it doesn't grow on trees.

Doctor Drivel's *Sensible* Household Tips

To remove stubborn coffee stains from a white shirt, soak it overnight in creosote.

Don't iron your curtains – you might fall out of the window.

Don't worry though, the ground will break your fall.

If you're rich and famous and love your wife, don't buy her a Jaguar. It might eat her.

If you take some medicine but forget to shake the bottle, jump up and down for a while.

If your budgerigar seems constipated, give it Chirrup of Figs.

If you want to stop your dog digging up the lawn, take his spade away.

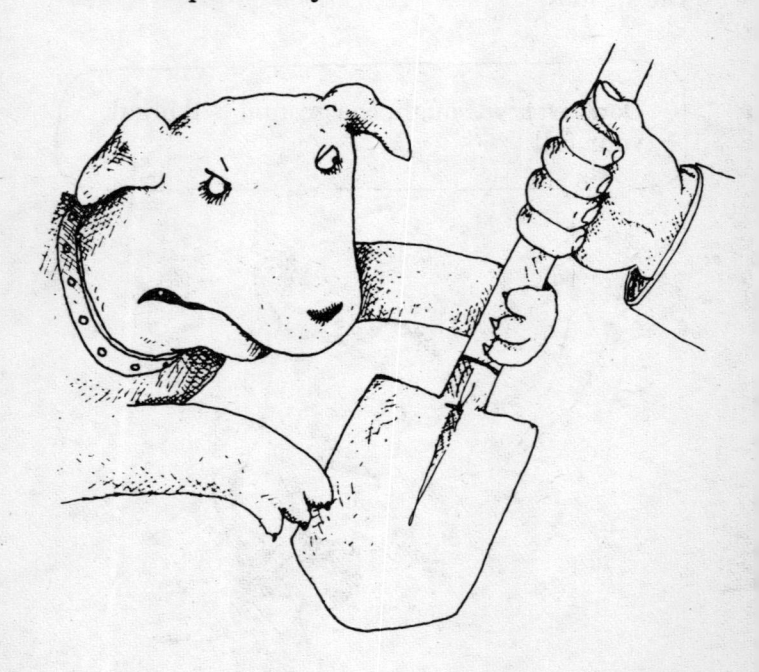

Make tea the easy way! Put the tea bag in your mouth, and drink a cup of boiling water.

Don't put manure on rhubarb. Custard tastes better.

If the brakes don't work on your car, drive home quickly before you have an accident.

Don't make fun of snakes – they don't like having their legs pulled.

To stop a fish from smelling, hold its nose.

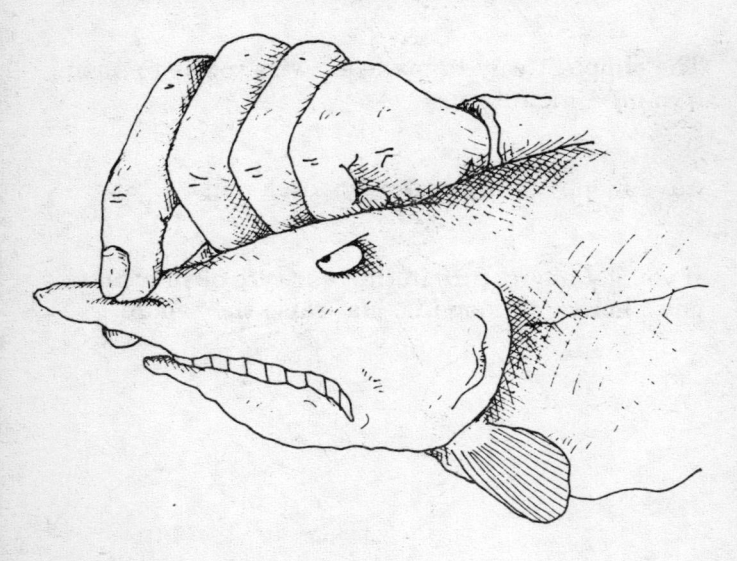

Chewing gum is not a good alternative to smoking cigarettes — it's too difficult to light.

Save money on your telephone bill — phone your friends when they're out.

To dial the Australian police, ring 666.

To make your own anti-freeze, shut her in the fridge.

If you want a flea circus you'll have to start from scratch.

The simplest way to make a Swiss roll is to push him off a mountain.

Save money — use waterproof tea bags.

If you get a puncture in the rear tyre of your bike, don't bother to mend it, just raise the saddle.

Seriously Puzzling Thoughts

If you snore very loudly and wake yourself up, is it best to sleep in another room?

How come wasps get so much time off for picnics?

Is being a judge a trying job?

Does a giraffe have to stand on a chair to clean its teeth?

Do ghosts believe in people?

Are two rows of cabbages a dual cabbage way?

If you want to know how much a whale weighs, do you have to take it to a whale weigh station?

Is the head of Kleenex a hankie chief?

Would stuffing jelly in one ear and cake in the other make you a trifle deaf?

Are sheep pen pals?

Is a very small mother a minimum?

Why don't they make antiques like they used to?

Do bicycles refuse to stand up on their own because they're two tyred?

In the Middle Ages, if you wanted to learn how to fight, did you go to knight school?

And do parrots learn to talk at polytechnics?

Can a match box? I suppose a tin can.

Is a window an amazing device that allows you to see through brick walls?

Is a net just a lot of holes held together with string?

Is it very cold in New Zealand? The lamb from there is always frozen solid.

Do Frenchmen find their hats on blackberet bushes?

Doctor Drivel's *Serious* Sports Special

What football team sounds like an ice cream?
Aston Vanilla.

That's why they always get licked.

MAN: I went duck hunting the other day, but we didn't get any.
FRIEND: *Why not?*
MAN: I couldn't throw the dogs high enough.

When you're playing snooker, you'll find the game progresses faster if you remove that wooden triangle.

My skiing is going downhill.

Water skiing would be more popular if there was more sloping water.

The English cricket team has stopped smoking.
Why?
They've lost all their matches.
[**Please note** : This joke only works after certain cricket seasons.]

Here's a very sensible joke about everyone's favourite sport — fishing.

An Eskimo was fishing one day through a hole in the ice. He was amazed when suddenly there was a loud booming voice that seemed to come from the sky all around him: 'THERE ARE NO FISH UNDER THE ICE,' it said.

The Eskimo was quite overcome; it was as if God was speaking directly to him!

'Is . . . that you . . . God?' he asked in a nervous voice.

'NO,' said the loud voice again, 'IT'S THE ICE RINK MANAGER!'

Now For Something Really *Serious*

> Probably the most absolutely SERIOUS joke in the whole history of the world is:

Why did the chicken cross the road?
To get to the other side.

> I'm sure you'll agree it's a fowl joke.

Here are some other versions, all of them are utterly, completely and totally sensible — well, give or take a few!

Why did the dog cross the road?
It was the chicken's day off.

Why did the turkey cross the road?
To show that he wasn't chicken.

Why did the dinosaur cross the road?
Chickens hadn't been invented then.

Why did the blind chicken cross the road?
To get to the Bird's Eye shop.

Why did the punk cross the road?
He was chained to the chicken.

Why did the man with one arm cross the road?
To get to the second hand shop.

Why did the Belgian man cross the road?
There's not much else to do in Belgium.

Why did the hedgehog cross the road?
To see his flat mate.

Why did the tortoise cross the road?
To get to the Shell garage.

Doctor Drivel at the Art Gallery

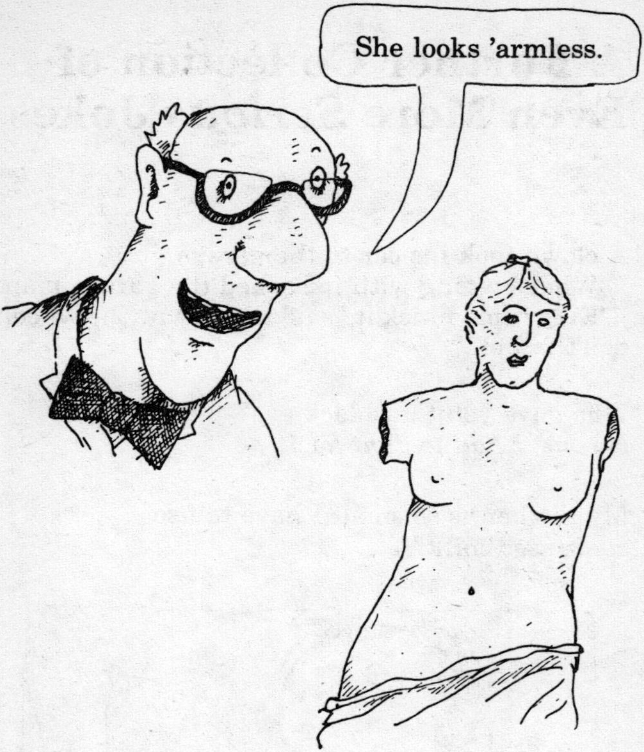
She looks 'armless.

A Further Collection of Even More *Serious* Jokes

A clown took his car to the garage.
'What's wrong with it?' asked the garage man.
'Everytime I kick it,' said the clown, 'the wheels don't fall off.'

Who gave you that black eye?
No one, I had to fight for it.

My kitchen is so small I have to use condensed milk.'

WOMAN: 'Yesterday I fell off a sixty foot ladder.'
FRIEND: *That's amazing: you were very lucky not to be killed.'*
WOMAN: 'Not really, I was only on the second rung!'

A man was run-over by a steamroller. He recovered in hospital, in wards 12, 13, 14, and 15.

A lady went into a workshop and saw a man hanging from the ceiling by one hand. 'What on earth is he doing? she asked one of the workers.
'Oh take no notice of him, he thinks he's a light bulb,' the worker explained.
'Well, shouldn't you get him down?' asked the lady, worried.
'What, and work in the dark?' the other replied.

A woman was looking very miserable.
'What's the matter?' asked her friend.
'My husband has made me into a millionaire,' said the woman.
'Why are you looking so sad then?'
'Before I met him I was a multi-millionaire.'

CUSTOMER (*in hardware shop*): A mousetrap please, and hurry, I've got a bus to catch.
SHOP ASSISTANT: *I'm sorry, Sir, we haven't got any that big.*

A man returned to a fish and chip shop. 'I don't think this fish is cooked,' he said to the man behind the counter.
'Why not?' asked the angry chef.
'It's just eaten my chips!' said the man.

A dude of a cowboy got on his horse facing the tail!

'You doggorn critter!' said another, 'You're facing the wrong way!'

'Shut up – you don't even know which way I want to go!' replied the dude.

Doctor Drivel's Doggorn Sensible Jokes

LITTLE GIRL: I call my new puppy Handyman.
HER FRIEND: *Why?*
LITTLE GIRL: He does little jobs about the house.

'What does a dog do on three legs,
that a man does standing up,
that a woman does sitting down?
Shakes hands!

For Sale: 'Dachshund puppies – Ideal draught excluders.'

There must be a lot of criminal sheep dogs around – they're always being sent to trials.

A man was eating some fish and chips at a bus stop. A lady came up with a little dog that kept yapping at the man and jumping up at his fish and chips.

'Can I throw him a bit?' the man asked the dog's owner.

'Certainly,' she replied.

So the man picked the dog up and threw it over a wall!

A crowd gathered in a pub round a man who was playing chess with his dog. 'That's just amazing!' said one of the onlookers.
'Not really,' said the man, looking up from the chess board.
'This is our tenth game and he's only beaten me twice!'

'Your dog has just chased a man on a bicycle.'
That's impossible, my dog can't ride a bicycle.

'Mum, can I have a puppy for Christmas?'
'No, dear, you'll have turkey like the rest of us.'

Where do you find a dog with no legs?
Wherever you left it.

A man went into a police station and told the officer on duty that he had lost his dog.

'Have you tried putting an advert in the newspaper?' asked the officer.

'That wouldn't work,' replied the man. 'My dog can't read!'

What's a police dog's phone number?
Canine, canine, canine.

A man came home with a very old looking dog.
'What's that?' asked his wife.
'It's a greyhound,' said the man. 'I'm going to race it.'
'By the look of it,' said his wife, 'you'll win?'

Yet More *Serious* Jokes

'How do you keep a really stupid person in suspense?'
'I don't know . . .'
'I'll tell you next week.'

MAN ON DOORSTEP: 'I'm collecting for the old folks' home.'
LITTLE GIRL: *'Hang on, I'll go and get my Grandad.'*

Famous *serious* last words

Bank robber: OK, stick 'em down.

Test pilot: What does this button do.

A lady wrote a letter to her ex-boyfriend.
Dear John, I missed you when you called at the house yesterday. Please come round again tomorrow so that I can have another shot.

A robber took his girlfriend out for the evening. After going to the cinema they walked down the high street hand in hand. They stopped outside a jewellers. 'Look at that lovely ring, Harry, I'd love that!'

'OK,' said Harry, and he bunged a brick through the window. He grabbed the ring and gave it to her as they ran off down the road.

Next they came to a fur shop. 'Look at that lovely fur coat Harry,' said the girl. 'I'd love that!'

'OK,' said Harry, and he threw a brick through the window and took the coat.

Then they came to a car show room. There in the window was a lovely white RollsRoyce. 'I'd love that car Harry,' said the girl.

'Hang on,' said Harry. 'What do you think I am? Made of bricks!!'

What do you call the man in charge of the cloak room in an Indian Restaurant?
Mahatma Coat.

Did you hear about the lady with five legs?
Her knickers fitted like a glove.

My brother does great farmyard impressions – he smells.

Did you hear about the Olympic fencing team?
They ran out of creosote.

A man came home drunk, with a pig under his arm.
'Where did you pick up that pig?' demanded his wife.
'Well. Ish like vish . . .' said the man.
'I'm not talking to you!' snapped his wife.

A rather serious farmer had difficulty telling the difference between two of his cows, but when he got out a tape measure he found that, sure enough, the brown one was two inches bigger than the white one.

A man went up to another serious farmer who was standing under a sign that said 'Pick Your Own Fruit'. 'I'd like to pick some fruit please,' said the man.
'Well do like the sign says,' said the farmer grumpily, 'Push off and pick your own – you're not picking mine!'

GIRL: Peter, you're stupid!
HER DAD: *That's a very unkind thing to say to your brother, say you're sorry.*
GIRL: Peter, I'm sorry you're stupid!

FIRST WAR VETERAN: My wooden leg is giving me a lot of pain.
SECOND WAR VETERAN: *Why?*
FIRST WAR VETERAN: My wife keeps hitting me over the head with it.

Doctor Drivel's Don't Get Cross Selection

What do you get if you cross an Australian cat with a roast duck?
A Duckfilled Fattypuss.

What do you get if you cross a giraffe with a hedgehog?
A hair brush with a very long handle.

What do you get if you cross a motorway with a skateboard?
Run over.

What do you get if you cross a skunk with a boomerang?
A smell that's very difficult to get rid of.

If you cross a skunk with an owl, do you get a bird that smells but doesn't give a hoot?

What do you get if you cross a fox with a chicken?
A fox.

What do you get if you cross a famous cowboy with an octopus?
Billy the Squid.

What do you get if you cross a famous warrior with a chicken?
Attila the Hen.

What do you get if you cross the Atlantic ocean with the Titanic?
About half way.

MAN: I met a very fierce woman dressed in black once.
FRIEND: *Really?*
MAN: Yes, Attila the Nun!

What do you get if you cross a hyena with a parrot?
An animal that laughs at its own jokes!

What do you get if you cross a robber with a cement mixer?
A hardened criminal.
[Please note: Cross a hen with a cement mixer and you get a brick-layer.]

Have you heard about the hyena that ate a box of Oxo cubes and made a laughing stock of itself?

What do you get if you cross a parrot with a python?
I don't know, but I wouldn't say 'who's a pretty boy then' to it.

If you cross a rose with an alligator you get a flower that bites your head off when you smell it.

What do you get if you cross an Englishman with a gallon of Australian beer?
A tiddly Pom.

What do you get if you cross a teddy bear with a skunk.
Winnie the Pooh.

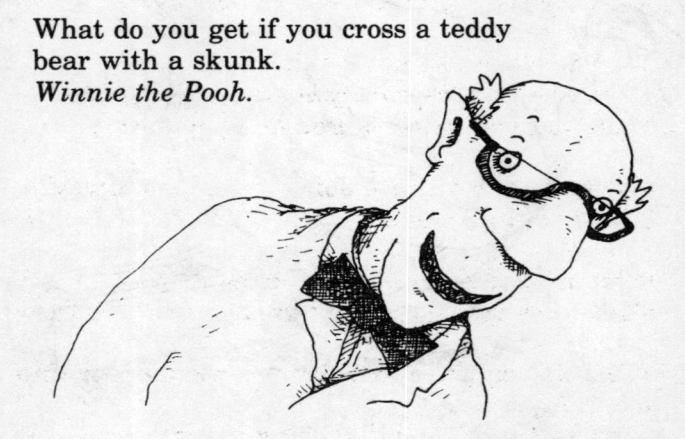

Serious Animal Corner

The easiest way to hire a horse is to stand it on four bricks.

If you find an injured wasp, take it to a waspital.

What's the difference between a cow and a bison?
You can't wash your hands in a cow.

What's grey, with four legs and a trunk?
An elephant?
No, a mouse going on holiday.

Well, what's *brown* with four legs and a trunk?
I don't know.
A mouse *coming back* from its holiday.

Why do elephants have wrinkles?
I don't know, why do elephants have wrinkles?
Have you ever tried to iron an elephant?

What was the tortoise doing on the motorway?
About a mile a week.

Why are kangeroos short of money?
When they grow up, they become out of pocket.

What do you get if you cross an elephant with a mouse?
Very big holes in your skirting boards.

What would you call Bambi if he went blind?
No eye deer.

What would you call him if you tied his legs together?
Still no eye deer.

What do you call a young sheep with a machine gun?
Lambo.

An elephant met a mouse.
  'How come I'm so big and strong, and you are so week and weedy?' demanded the elephant.
  'Well, I haven't been very well recently,' said the mouse.

What did the elephant say when the crocodile bit it's trunk off?
'I subbose you fink dat's funny.'

If you cross a creature from a Scottish lake, with a man who never wins anything, you get the Luckless Monster.

Doctor Drivel's Guide To *Serious* Tourists

Doctor Drivel: The other day I was waiting to cross the road at a pedestrian crossing, and when the lights changed it started to bleep — bee-bee-bee-bee-.

'What's that noise?' asked an American tourist standing next to me.

'That's to let blind people know that the lights have changed,' I said, very politely.

'Oh *my*!' said the American, 'In our country we don't let blind people drive cars!'

An American tourist was going round London in a taxi: 'Say driver — what's that building there?'

'That's Buckingham Palace.'

'We can put up buildings like that in three weeks back home. What's that building?'

'That's Westminster Abbey, Sir,' said the taxi driver, beginning to get cross.

'Say, we put up buildings like that in two weeks back home. What's that building?' the American asked, pointing at the Houses of Parliament.

'I don't know,' said the driver. 'It wasn't there this morning.'

An American tourist drove in to an English village and went into the pub. He got talking to an old villager in the bar. 'Say, have you lived here all your life?' he asked.

'Not yet,' said the old man.

Another tourist asked an old villager who was the oldest man in the village.

'No one at the moment,' said the villager. 'The one we had died last week!'

Doctor Drivel's Guide to Frogs

Now: Two frog's legs jokes for the price of one!

MAN (*in restaurant*): Waiter, do you have frog's legs?
ANSWER NUMBER ONE: *No Sir, I always walk like this.*
ANSWER NUMBER TWO: *Yes Sir.*
MAN: Well hop off to the kitchen and get me a steak!

Doctor Drivel: As you can see from all these jokes, frogs are fairly serious little creatures.

Here is the news: A frog threw itself off a skyscraper this morning — the police say it Kermitted suicide.

Another frog's car broke down on the motorway. It had to be toad away.

Where do frogs go to the lavatory?
In the croak-room.

What's green and dangerous?
A frog with a submachine gun.

The Writing's not on the Wall

Doctor Drivel: Graffiti can be seriously serious, especially when it's on a wall. This graffiti is not so completely seriously serious — because it's in a book.

I don't like graffiti, in fact I don't really like any Italian food

I used to be indecisive, but now I'm not so sure

The Queen Rules UK

Florists Rule — bouquet!

The Meek Rule — if that's all right with everybody else.

Twelve Inches Rule, OK

I used to be schizophrenic, but now I'm in two minds about it

The Spanish Rule, Ole!

I was a kleptomaniac, but I took something for it

Don't vote — the government will get in

Insanity is hereditary — you get it from your children

Tolkien is Hobbit-forming

When I was younger I had a terrible experience. I met a sub-human alien monster.
Did you tell the police?
No, I married it!

Doctor Drivel's Sensible Children's Corner

Mum!
What is it dear?
Can I have a glass of water please.
But I've just brought you up one.
I know, but my bedroom's on fire.

Eat your breakfast dear, you can't go to school on an empty stomach.
I'm not going to, I'm going on my bike.

A little old lady stopped a passing Boy Scout and said, 'Excuse me young man, can you see me across the road?'

'Hang on,' said the Scout, 'I'll go over and have a look.'

MOTHER: Eat up your cabbage Jennifer, it will put colour into your cheeks.
JENNIFER: *I don't want green cheeks!*

'Dad, if I say that when I grow up I want to drive a steamroller, would you stand in my way?'

BARBER: Would you like a haircut?
BOY (*in chair*): *I'd like them all cut!*
BARBER: And how would you like it cut?
BOY: *Shorter!*

TEACHER: Go and stand at the end of the line.
BOY: *I can't, there's someone there already!*

Girl (home from school): Bad news Dad, you got my homework wrong again!

Boy (home from school): Good news Dad – you know you said you'd give me ten pounds for every exam I passed? I've just saved you a lot of money!

FIRST BOY: Can you come out to play?
SECOND BOY: *No, I've got to help Mum with my homework.*

Mummy Mummy! There's Something *Seriously* Wrong

Mummy Mummy, I don't want to go to America!
Shut up, and keep swimming.

Mummy Mummy, I'm a vegetarian.
Shut up, and drink your soup before it congeals.

Mummy Mummy, what's a werewolf?
Shut up and comb your face.

Mummy Mummy, can I start wearing a bra?
Shut up Henry.

Mummy Mummy, why do I keep walking in circles?
Shut up or I'll get your dad to nail your other foot to the floor.

Mummy Mummy, what's for dinner?
Shut up and get back in the oven.

Doctor Drivel's Very Own Sensible Knock Knock Jokes

KNOCK! KNOCK!

There's someone at the door with a wooden leg.
Tell him to hop it.

There's a woman at the door with a pram.
Tell her to push off.

There's a bee keeper at the door.
Tell him to buzz off.

There's a man at the door with a bill.
Tell him we've already got some.

The Invisible Man's at the door.
Tell him I can't see him now.

There's someone at the door with a drum.
Tell him to beat it.

Here is the News

Rather very serious news at that.

DRIVEL NEWS

Archaeologists have discovered the bones of a very short-sighted dinosaur; it will be called a Doyouthinkhesawus.

A lorry loaded with hair restorer overturned today on the M1. Police are combing the area.

Another lorry loaded with glue overturned on the M2. Police are asking drivers to stick to their own lanes.

A barman died today. The police will hold an inn-quest.

Police are looking for a man with one leg called Johnstone. They don't know what his other leg is called.

A ship loaded with yo-yos sank forty-three times in the channel today.

A plastic surgeon stood too close to a fire today. He melted. His friends said that he had made a complete pool of himself.

[**Please note**: It's a bit like the optician who took all his clothes off in the street and made a spectacle of himself.]

A man has succeeded in crossing a retriever dog with a tortoise. He's bred an animal that goes down to the corner shop, and comes back with last week's paper.

Police have arrested some prunes for being stewed. They are being held in custardy.

A particularly serious man put his false teeth in the wrong way round this morning, and ate himself.

The police say that the M6 will be closed today. Motorists who intended to use it should now use the M3 twice.

A man had reported being mugged by two men. One was six feet three inches tall, the other was a dwarf. The police are hunting high and low for them.

A man has escaped from prison during a heat wave. The police think he broke out in a sweat.

Another man escaped and is thought to have eaten three boxes of prunes. The police are looking for a man on the run.

Football results:
Finland 2, Fatland 4

Shooting results:
Bagshot 4, Aldershot 1

Doctor Drivel's Own List of *Seriously* Sensible Things to do

Run a restaurant that closes for lunch

Put the cat out, when it's not even on fire.

Take up Morris dancing, but be careful you don't fall off the bonnet.

Take up tap dancing – you can practise in the bathroom.

If you are fishing from a hired boat on a lake, and you start to catch lots of fish, don't chalk a cross on the side of the boat so that you can find the same spot again – you might get a different boat next time.

Take a crash course in car driving.

If you're walking along the beach with your girlfriend, and she says, 'Look, a dead seagull', look up into the sky and say, 'Where?'

If your granny says she'd like to rock and roll, fit skates to her rocking chair.

If you want to have fun and cut your toe nails at the same time, learn to sword dance.

One of the Most *Serious* Topics in the World – Teachers

ANGRY TEACHER: I'm going to give you a piece of my mind!
CHEEKY GIRL: *I didn't know you had any to spare.*

'Teachers are great – they're in a class of their own.'
'Yes, but cross-eyed ones can't control their pupils!'

A boy came back from school with his report. 'What are your results like?' asked his mum.

'Well,' said the boy thoughtfully, 'they could have been worse; I came bottom out of thirty-two.'

'How could that have been worse?' asked his mother, horrified.

'There could have been more children in the class,' said the boy.

A girl came home from school. 'What were your exam results like, dear?' asked her dad.

'They were a bit wet,' said the girl.

'What do you mean?'

'They were all below C level!' said the girl, and then she made a run for it.

School report: Despite strong competition he has retained his position at the bottom of the class.

ANGRY TEACHER: How ever can you make so many maths mistakes in one day?
BOY: *I get up early.*

SCHOOL SECRETARY, (*on phone*): I'm very sorry Mrs Jones, but young Robert has swallowed a fifty pence piece.
MRS JONES: *That's all right, it was his dinner money.*

A cruel teacher gave a girl detention for something she didn't do. Her homework!

TEACHER: During the maths exam you may use pocket calculators.
BOY: *I won't need to – I know how many pockets I've got!*

Doctors! – Oh No, How *Serious*

Doctor, doctor, I've got terrible wind. Can you give me something for it!
Sure – here's a kite.

A woman was putting on her coat.

'Where are you going Mum,' asked her little daughter.

'I'm taking your brother to the doctors. I don't like the look of him.'

'I don't like the look of him either,' replied the girl.

PATIENT: Doctor there's something wrong with my eyes.
DOCTOR: *Yes, I think you've got double vision.*
PATIENT: I'm not taking any notice of you two, I want a third opinion!
Please note: There's a really sensible new cure for double vision: closing one eye.

'Doctor, what do you think is causing this pain in my right leg?' asked an elderly patient.

'I think it's just age,' said the doctor.

'But my left leg is the same age as the right one, and it doesn't hurt a bit!' replied the man.

A man went to the doctor. 'Right,' said the doc, 'I want you to go home and take this medicine, followed by a nice warm bath.'

A week later the man returned. 'How did you get on?' asked the doctor kindly.

'Well,' said the man, 'I took the medicine, but I just couldn't manage to drink all the bath.'

Doctor, I'm really worried. I think I'm turning into a dog.
Well, sit down and tell me all about it.
I can't, I'm not allowed on the furniture.

Doctor doctor, I think I'm a pair of curtains.
Well pull yourself together.

Doctor doctor, I think I'm an apple.
Well sit down, I won't bite you.

Doctor doctor, I think I'm a bridge.
Now then, what's come over you?
So far three cars and a lorry.

Doctor doctor, I'm at death's door.
Don't worry, we'll pull you through.

Doctor doctor, I think I'm a billiard ball.
Well wait at the end of the queue.

You see . . . cue, very clever, very sensible.

Doctor doctor I've only got 59 seconds to live!
Sit over there, I'll see you in a minute.

Doctor doctor, everyone ignores me.
Next!

DOCTOR: Now Mr Smith, I've got some good news and some bad news, which do you want first?
MR SMITH: *The bad news Doctor.*
DOCTOR: The bad news is that I'm going to have to cut both your legs off.
MR SMITH: *What's the good news?*
DOCTOR: The good news is that the man in the next bed would like to buy your slippers.

Doctor, it's terrible, my husband thinks he's a chicken.
Why didn't you tell me this before?
We needed the eggs!

Doctor doctor, I think I'm a goat.
How long have you felt like this!
Since I was a kid.

Doctor doctor, I think I've lost my memory.
When did this start?
When did what start?

Doctor doctor, it's terrible, my wife thinks she's a swallow!
Oh dear, you'd better tell her to come and see me.
I can't she's, flown south for the winter.

Doctor doctor, I'm shrinking.
Well you'll just have to be a little patient!

A man went to the doctor and said that he had begun to be able to see into the future.
　'When did this start?' asked the doctor.
　'Next Thursday!' said the man.

Doctor doctor, I think I need glasses.
You certainly do – this is a fish and chip shop!

PATIENT: I feel really ill, my nose is dripping, my eyes are running, my chest's all clogged up. Can you help me?
DOCTOR: *No, why not try a plumber?*

Doctor Drivel Asks a Very Sensible Question: What Do You Call. . . ?

What do you call a man who comes through your letter box every morning?
Bill.

What do you call a woman who sets fire to her bills?
Bernadette.

Burn-a-debt, get it?

What do you call a woman who goes into a pub and juggles with the drinks?
Beatrix.

Beer tricks — and if she then starts playing snooker she's probably Beatrix Potter!

What do you call a girl with eggs and bacon on her head?
Kaff.

What do you call a girl with slates on her head?
Ruth.

What do you call a man who swims in circles in a river?
Eddy.

What do you call a man with rabbits down his trousers?
Warren.

What do you call a woman who clings to the sides of old buildings?
Ivy.

What do you call a woman with one leg shorter than the other?
Eileen.

Very serious – I lean!

What do you call a man with a plank of wood on his head?
Edward.
Three planks and it's probably Edward Woodward.

What do you call a girl who lies across the middle of a tennis court?
Annette.

What do you call a woman with one foot on either side of a river?
Bridget.

What do you call a man with an elephant on his head?
Squashed.

Everyone knows that you call a man with a seagull on his head Cliff, but did you hear about the man who went into a doctor's surgery with a seagull on his head?

'What seems to be the trouble?' asked the doctor.

'I've got this man stuck to my feet,' said the seagull!

What do you call a man with a banana in one ear and a sausage in the other?
Anything – he can't hear you!

What do you call a girl with a bus on her head?
Uncomfortable.

Doctor Drivel's Christmas Crackers.

Christmas can be a particularly serious time of the year.

'My mum asked Dad for something with diamonds in it for Christmas: he bought her a pack of cards!'

Liverpool have just signed a new player who insists on wearing black wellies, a red cloak with a hood, and a large false beard. The club say he will be their new Santa Forward.

A woman took her son to the doctors because he was very frightened of Father Christmas coming down the chimney. 'It's a bad case of Santa-klaustrophobia,' said the doctor.

WIFE: I'd like some crocodile shoes for Christmas.
HUSBAND: *OK, what size does the crocodile take?*

FARMER: I've bred some turkeys that will make my fortune at Christmas — they've got three legs.
HIS FRIEND: *What do they taste like?*
FARMER: I don't know, I haven't been able to catch one yet!

Doctor Drivel's *Serious* Restaurant Guide

A man had just finished a rather mingy meal.
 'Thank you, Sir,' said the waiter, taking his plate away. 'How did you find your steak?'
 'I just moved a lettuce leaf and there it was!' said the man.

Waiter, call me a taxi!
Certainly; you are a taxi, Sir.

Waiter, there's a fly in my soup.
So that's where they go in the winter.

Waiter, does the band do requests?
Yes, Sir.
Good, go and ask them to play next door.

Waiter, you've got your big greasy thumb on my steak.
I know, Sir, but you wouldn't want it to fall on the floor again would you?.

Waiter, there's a fly in my soup.
Don't worry, it won't live long in that stuff, Sir.

Waiter, do you serve lobsters?
We'll serve anyone — sit where you like, Sir.

A man in a restaurant spilled soup into his lap.
'Waiter!' he yelled. 'I've got soup in my flies!'

Waiter, will my pancake be long?
No, Sir, it will be round.

Waiter, what's this fly doing in my soup?
Backstroke, Sir.

Serious Book Titles

Doctor Drivel: If you thought *this* book had a sensible title, you should read some of these!

Great Shipwrecks by Mandy Lifeboats

Falling off a Cliff by Eileen Dover

Chinese Windowcleaning by Hoo Flung Dung

Silver Wedding by Annie Versary

Get Rich Quick by Robin Banks

Say Your Prayers by Neil Down

Great Murders by U Dunnit

Walking the Plank by Hugo First

By Boat to The North Pole by I C Waters

Carpet Fitting by Walter Wall

Doctor Drivel's *Serious* Cookery Corner

To stop rice sticking together when you cook it — boil each grain separately.

To make an apple turnover – push it down a hill.

[**Please note:** You can make a sausage roll like this too.]

To make a cream puff – chase it round the garden.

Other great reads from Red Fox

Further Red Fox titles that you might enjoy reading are listed on the following pages. They are available in bookshops or they can be ordered directly from us.

If you would like to order books, please send this form and the money due to:

ARROW BOOKS, BOOKSERVICE BY POST, PO BOX 29, DOUGLAS, ISLE OF MAN, BRITISH ISLES. Please enclose a cheque or postal order made out to Arrow Books Ltd for the amount due, plus 22p per book for postage and packing, both for orders within the UK and for overseas orders.

NAME _____

ADDRESS _____

_____

Please print clearly.

Whilst every effort is made to keep prices low, it is sometimes necessary to increase cover prices at short notice. If you are ordering books by post, to save delay it is advisable to phone to confirm the correct price. The number to ring is THE SALES DEPARTMENT 071 (if outside London) 973 9700.

Other great reads from **Red Fox**

The latest and funniest joke books are from Red Fox!

THE OZONE FRIENDLY JOKE BOOK
Kim Harris, Chris Langham, Robert Lee, Richard Turner

What's green and highly dangerous?
How do you start a row between conservationists?
What's green and can't be rubbed out?

Green jokes for green people (non-greens will be pea-green when they see how hard you're laughing), bags and bags of them (biodegradable of course).

All the jokes in this book are printed on environmentally friendly paper and every copy you buy will help GREENPEACE save our planet.

* David Bellamy with a machine gun.
* Pour oil on troubled waters.
* The Indelible hulk.

ISBN 0 09 973190 8   £1.99

THE HAUNTED HOUSE JOKE BOOK
John Hegarty

There are skeletons in the scullery . . .
Beasties in the bath . . .
There are spooks in the sitting room
And jokes to make you laugh . . .

Search your home and see if we are right. Then come back, sit down and shudder to the hauntingly funny and eerily rib-rattling jokes in this book.

ISBN 0 09 9621509   £1.99